# HE GUYS GUIDE TO MAKING LIFE MORE AWESOME

BY ERIC BRAUN

capstone
young readers

# TABLE OF CONTENTS

# LIFE IS AN ADVENTURE!

Life can be an awesome adventure! You just need to know where to start. That's what this book is for. It's full of awesome ideas to have more fun and improve your skills. You can learn how to throw a perfect spiral pass, survive in the wild, explore a city, or even make a stop-motion movie! You'll be inspired by the incredible adventures and amazing achievements of others. And when you're done reading, you can show your friends how to have awesome adventures of their own.

You don't have to be a super genius or a popular athlete. What matters is finding the awesomeness hidden inside of you. It's up to you to make your life as awesome as it can be!

# TOP THINGS EVERY GUY NEEDS

Every guy needs some basic stuff to get the most out of every experience. Some of these things can be found at the store. But others will come from inside of you.

## A NOTEBOOK AND PEN OR PENCIL

Write down stuff you want to remember, such as your creative ideas, cool stuff you see, or books you want to read.

## A SENSE OF HUMOR

The world can be hilarious. Look for the humor in everything, and share the laughs with others.

## GENEROSITY

Sharing your stuff is great. But you can also be generous with your time and your attitudes toward others.

## GOOD FRIENDS

Good friends are those people you can trust in any situation. You know you can count on them to share in your adventures or to keep your secrets.

## A RELIABLE ADULT

People with life experience can help you with the big questions in life. Whether it's your dad or mom, your grandfather, or an uncle, a trusted adult is a great source of support whenever you need someone to talk to.

## A SENSE OF ADVENTURE

The right mind-set can go a long way. With a positive attitude and an adventurous spirit, you can make good experiences amazing.

## A ROLL OF DUCT TAPE

Duct tape is some of the most useful stuff ever invented. Keep a roll nearby. You never know when it might come in handy.

## A MULTI-PURPOSE POCKET KNIFE

A good multi-purpose pocket knife is one of the most useful things you can own. Make sure it has screwdrivers and other useful tools.

## PERSISTENCE

Awesome things in life don't always come easy. Remember, trying your hardest is what makes you a great guy, not being perfect.

## A SMILE

It's been proven that smiling can help you feel happier. It also helps others relax and creates a positive impression of you.

# MAKE SPORTS MORE AWESOME!

Across the court, your opponent is bent over and breathing hard. It's been a tough battle. But when your eyes meet his, he gives you a smile. His team is up by three points. He thinks they've got it in the bag. Your teammate passes the basketball inbounds to you. You turn toward the basket with only six seconds left on the clock. What do you do?

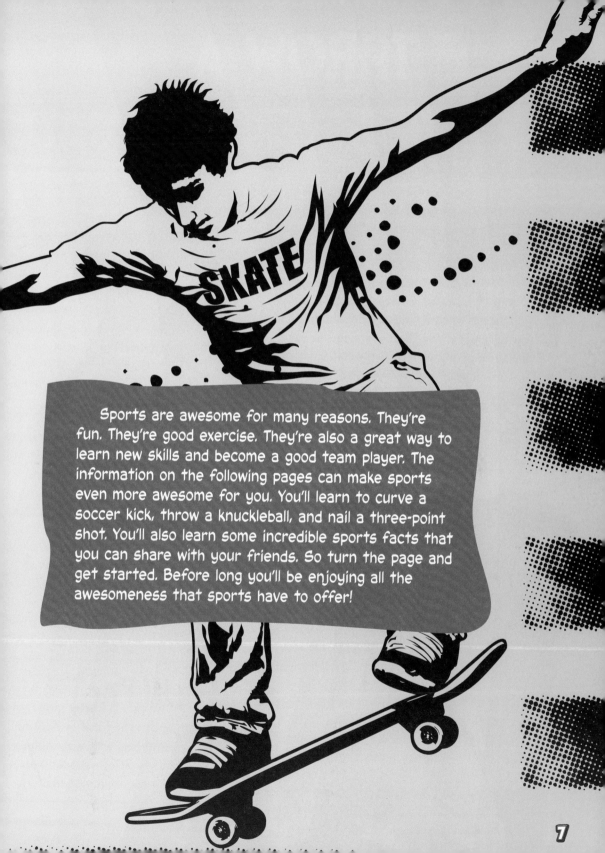

Sports are awesome for many reasons. They're fun. They're good exercise. They're also a great way to learn new skills and become a good team player. The information on the following pages can make sports even more awesome for you. You'll learn to curve a soccer kick, throw a knuckleball, and nail a three-point shot. You'll also learn some incredible sports facts that you can share with your friends. So turn the page and get started. Before long you'll be enjoying all the awesomeness that sports have to offer!

# THROW A
# DAZZLING KNUCKLEBALL

The batter takes a swing—and misses! A well-thrown knuckleball is very difficult to hit. In a knuckleball pitch, the ball barely spins after you release it. Air pushes the ball in different directions so it wobbles as it floats toward the batter.

**1** Grip the ball with your thumb on the bottom and your fingertips on top. Place your fingertips against the horseshoe–shaped seam in the ball.

**2** Wind up as if you are going to throw a typical fastball. Keep the ball hidden in your glove for as long as possible. You don't want the batter to see how you're holding the ball.

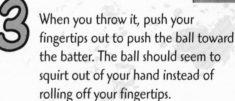

**3** When you throw it, push your fingertips out to push the ball toward the batter. The ball should seem to squirt out of your hand instead of rolling off your fingertips.

## FUN FACT:

Major League Baseball (MLB) pitcher R. A. Dickey won the National League Cy Young Award in 2012. Almost all of his pitches are knuckleballs.

# THROW A
# PERFECT SPIRAL

Footballs have an odd, oblong shape. It's easy to make wobbly passes that miss the receiver. Learn to throw a good spiral pass, and you'll have a better chance of hitting the target.

**1** Hold the ball about two-thirds of the way back with your fingers on the laces. This will give you control and power on your pass.

**2** Stand with your feet about shoulder-width apart. Hold the ball in both hands at chest level.

**3** Step toward your target with your lead leg. Your non-throwing shoulder should also face toward the target. At the same time, bring your throwing arm back.

**4** When you throw the ball, drop your lead elbow as you move your throwing arm forward. When you release the ball, your throwing arm should be fully extended toward your target.

**5** The key to a great spiral is in the release. As you release the ball, snap your wrist down so your thumb points toward the ground. To create spin, let the ball roll off your fingers. The tip of your index finger should be the last thing to touch the ball. Keep practicing until you've mastered the art of a perfect spiral pass.

# HOST A BIKE OLYMPICS

Take bike riding to the next level with a little competition. Gather your friends together to hold your own bike Olympics! You'll need a large open area, such as a parking lot. Try using the following events, or make up your own. Have fun, and be sure to always wear a helmet for safety.

## SPRINT RACE

Choose a short distance, such as 150 feet (46 meters). Mark off the start and finish lines. When you race, take off as fast as possible and go all out until the finish line.

## ENDURANCE RACE

Map out a long course through your neighborhood, or have riders go several laps around your block. The rider who completes the course in the fastest time wins.

## OBSTACLE COURSE

Use traffic cones, rope, boxes, or chalk lines to make an obstacle course. Time each rider as he goes through it. The fastest time wins.

# THE INCREDIBLE STING-RAY

Schwinn introduced the Sting-Ray bicycle in 1963. The Sting-Ray featured high handlebars, a banana seat, and a close wheelbase. Its design was different from previous bikes. Kids soon learned that the Sting-Ray was perfect for doing wheelies and bunny hops, as well as racing on dirt courses. The Sting-Ray eventually led to today's popular BMX bikes, races, and stunts.

## PAPERBOY CONTEST

Hang a Hula-Hoop from a tree branch or some playground equipment. Riders score points by throwing tennis balls or rolled-up newspapers through the hoop as they ride by. If the score is tied, move the riders farther from the hoop.

## BUNNY HOP CONTEST

Stand a piece of plywood upright on the ground. Then have riders hop their bikes as they ride past the board. Mark the height of each rider's jump on the board. The highest jumper wins!

## BIKE POLO

This event requires a lot of skill and should be played only by experienced riders. Teams of three, four, or five compete on a grass field or parking lot. Riders hit a street hockey ball with a bike polo mallet to try to score points. You can order a bike polo mallet on the Internet. Or you can build your own mallet with a ski pole and a piece of PVC pipe. Get an adult to help you build the mallet. Use traffic cones to set up goals at each end of the playing area.

## FIND A SPONSOR

You can make your bike Olympics an awesome public event by asking a bike shop to sponsor you. Use the bike shop's parking lot, or ask if they can set up the event at your local community center. Ask people from the shop to discuss safety equipment, safe riding tips, and bike maintenance. You can also ask for help organizing and advertising the event.

# CREATE AN AWESOME FANTASY LEAGUE

Sports fans love dramatic buzzer-beaters and last-second touchdowns. But there's a way to make your favorite sport even more fun—start your own fantasy league! In fantasy sports, people pick pro players for made-up teams that they manage themselves. Points are scored based on league rules and how players perform in real games. Try these tips to help your league stand out.

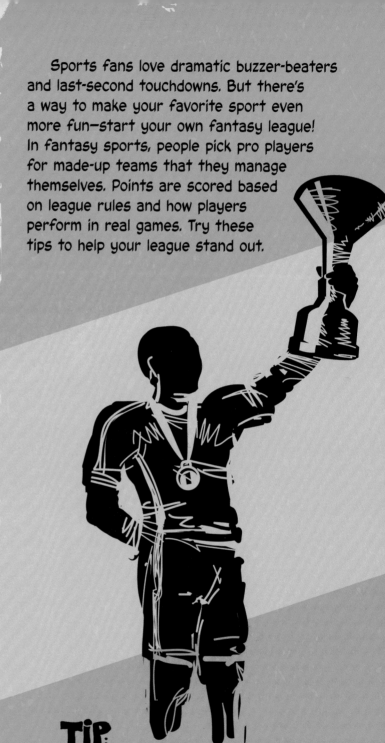

**TIP:**

Consider starting a fantasy league based on an obscure sport. Why not try fantasy BMX, fantasy chess, fantasy fishing, or fantasy lacrosse? Some people even play fantasy curling!

POP CORN

Invite all your friends to join your league. People don't need to be big sports fans to enjoy running a fantasy team. Just enjoying some friendly competition is half the fun.

Include an unusual scoring category. Make things interesting with different scoring systems. For example, maybe your fantasy football team can get extra points for fake field goals. Or try taking away points for penalties.

Do a live draft at someone's house. Fantasy sports are about spending time with friends. Grab some snacks, break out your cheat sheets, and get ready for some good-natured heckling with your buddies.

Try an auction league. In an auction league, everyone has a set amount of imaginary money. Team owners track the money they spend on each player. Once the money is gone, they can't get more players. It takes a skilled owner to get the best players for the least money.

It's fun to give your friends a hard time during the season. But be careful not to go too far. Do it in the spirit of fun and friendship. Nothing kills the fun like mean comments that hurt people's feelings.

# CURVE A
# SOCCER KICK

During a penalty kick in soccer, you can make the goalie's job difficult with a curved kick. With enough practice, you can even curve the ball into the net on a corner kick.

1. Approach the ball from a 45-degree angle.

2. Plant your non-kicking foot a little behind the ball. Then swing your kicking leg at an angle that will bring it across your body during the follow through.

3. With the inside of your kicking foot, begin the kick at the bottom outside corner of the ball. Move your foot diagonally toward the top inside corner of the ball.

4. During your follow through, turn your shoulders toward your target so your leg follows across your body.

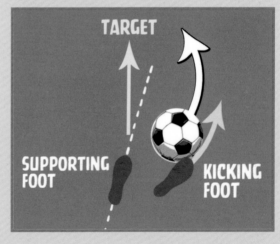

TARGET

SUPPORTING FOOT

KICKING FOOT

**GETTING A GREAT CURVED KICK TAKES A LOT OF PRACTICE.**

**DON'T GET DISCOURAGED!**

# OLLIE A SKATEBOARD

Ollie-oop! Experienced skateboarders know how to do a simple jump trick called an ollie. This cool move will have you hopping your board over stuff in no time.

1. Place your back foot on the board's tail end. Keep your front foot at the middle of the board.

2. As you roll forward, crouch down slightly, and then jump straight up. Raise your arms when you jump.

3. As you jump, slam down the tail of the board with your back foot. The nose of the board will bounce upward.

4. While in the air, slide your front foot forward to level out the board. At the same time, lift your back foot so the tail of the board can rise.

5. Be sure to keep your knees bent to help cushion your landing.

## FUN FACT:

Alan Gelfand invented the ollie in 1976 as a way to "get air" in empty swimming pools and skate bowls. In 1982 Rodney Mullen became the first skater to do an ollie on flat ground.

# BUILD A SKATE RAMP

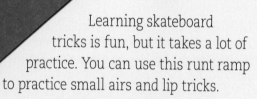

Learning skateboard tricks is fun, but it takes a lot of practice. You can use this runt ramp to practice small airs and lip tricks.

Be sure not to use power tools without an adult's help. If you get hurt, you'll be spending time in the hospital instead of on your skateboard.

## SUPPLIES

- 1 sheet of 3/4-inch (1.9-cm) plywood. 4 x 8 feet (1.2 x 2.4 m)
- 2 sheets of 1/4-inch (0.6-cm) plywood. 4 x 4 feet (1.2 x 1.2 m)
- 1 sheet of 1/8-inch (0.3-cm) hardboard. 4 x 6 feet (1.2 x 1.8 m)
- 13 boards 2 x 4 inches (5 x 10 cm). 4 feet (1.2 m) long

- 1 box of 2-inch (5-cm) nails with wide heads
- 1 box of 2 1/2-inch (6.4-cm) wood screws
- hammer
- jigsaw
- drill with screwdriver attachment
- helpful adult

# STEPS

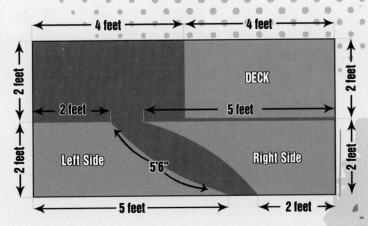

**1.** Mark out the two sides and deck of the ramp on the sheet of 3/4-inch plywood. Follow the measurements given here for each piece. Then with an adult's help, cut out the pieces with the jigsaw.

**2.** Connect the two side pieces by nailing 2 x 4 boards between them. Start with the corners of the deck and the bottom of the ramp. Then nail the remaining 2 x 4 boards between the sides about 8 inches (20 cm) apart.

**3.** Lay the deck piece on the support boards at the top of the ramp. Screw it into place along the outside edges. Be sure to always countersink the screws, making sure that the heads are below the surface of the wood.

**4.** Lay one sheet of 1/4-inch plywood into the curved ramp and screw it to the support boards. Then lay the second sheet of 1/4-inch plywood over the first and screw it down.

**5.** Finally, place the piece of hardboard onto the ramp and screw it down. It should overlap the end of the ramp and touch the ground. This will allow your skateboard to easily roll onto the ramp.

# GREAT SPORTS MOMENTS

Sports fans love watching their heroes' incredible achievements. History is filled with stories of athletes who overcame nearly impossible odds. Here are a few amazing and inspiring stories every sports fan should know.

## RUMBLE IN THE JUNGLE

One of boxing's most historic fights took place in Zaire, Africa. The 1974 match was nicknamed the "Rumble in the Jungle." The fight featured Muhammad Ali and George Foreman, who was the current champion. Many thought Foreman would win easily. However, Ali had a plan. He let Foreman unleash a string of huge punches, blocking most of them. Foreman soon grew tired. That's when Ali began landing his own punches. He knocked Foreman out in the eighth round. Ali later called his strategy the "rope-a-dope" method.

## WEIRD WAY TO WIN

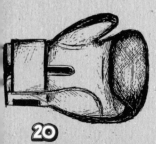

In a 1989 boxing match, light heavyweight champion Steve McCarthy had Tony Wilson up against the ropes. But then things got weird. Wilson's mom jumped into the ring and started whacking McCarthy with her shoe! McCarthy was cut on the head and unable to go on. The judges ended up giving the victory to Wilson.

# PERFECT IN THE POOL

At the 2008 Summer Olympics, hopes were sky-high for American swimmer Michael Phelps. In the 2004 Olympics, Phelps had won eight medals, including six golds. He had also broken five world records. Everybody was talking about what Phelps might do in 2008. But if he was nervous, he didn't show it. He won all of his events and set a record with eight gold medals in a single Olympics. Phelps went on to add another six medals during the 2012 Olympics. With a total of 22 career medals, Phelps is the most successful Olympic athlete of all time.

# RUNNING BACK ... ALL THE WAY BACK

Near the end of the 2011 season, Minnesota Vikings star running back Adrian Peterson suffered a major knee injury. Doctors repaired it, but they didn't think he'd be ready for the start of the 2012 season. However, Peterson said that he would be ready—and he was! He rushed for 84 yards and two touchdowns in his first game back. He went on to become only the seventh player in history to rush for more than 2,000 yards. In fact, with a total of 2,097 rushing yards, he came just nine yards short of breaking the single-season rushing record! Peterson topped off his amazing season by winning the 2012 NFL Most Valuable Player award.

# DEVASTATING

Almost everyone enjoys some kind of sport. However, being a sports fan can be a lot like riding on a roller coaster. There are plenty of ups and downs. Check out a few of the biggest heartbreaks sports fans have dealt with over the years.

## SUPER BUMMERS

In 1991 the Buffalo Bills were big favorites to win Super Bowl XXV. But they lost the game when Buffalo kicker Scott Norwood missed his last-second field goal attempt. Losing that game was bad enough, but it was only the beginning. The Bills went on to become the only team in history to go to four Super Bowls in a row. But sadly for Bills fans, the team lost every time.

## NO GOAL?

In 1999 the Buffalo Sabres were one game away from winning their first Stanley Cup title. But during the third overtime, Dallas Stars wing Brett Hull stuck his skate into the crease. He kicked the puck away from the goalie and then flipped it into the net. But when Hull scored, his skate was still in the crease, which was against the rules. However, the officials ruled that the goal was legal. To this day Sabres fans claim that Hull cheated to win the Stanley Cup. And Buffalo has still never won a championship.

# DISAPPOINTMENTS

## FAN INTERFERENCE

The Chicago Cubs have not won a national title since 1908. And they haven't been to a World Series since 1945. But in the 2003 National League Championship Series, they were just five outs away from going to the World Series. In the eighth inning of game six, a Florida Marlins batter popped a long foul ball toward left field. As the ball sailed toward the stands, Moises Alou tried to catch it. But several fans reached out for it too. One fan, Steve Bartman, deflected the ball so Alou couldn't make the catch. The Marlins went on to win that game and game seven to go to the World Series. Many Cubs fans feel that "The Bartman Game" proves that the team is cursed.

## THE CURSE OF THE BILLY GOAT

Cubs fans know a lot about curses. In 1945 a Cubs fan brought his pet goat into a World Series game. But he was kicked out because the goat smelled so bad. The angry fan declared, "Them Cubs, they ain't gonna win no more." The Cubs have not been back to the World Series since. The Curse of the Billy Goat seems to have stuck with the Cubs.

# INCREASE YOUR RUNNING SPEED

The fastest runners in the world can sprint 100 meters in less than 10 seconds! You may not break any records, but these tips can help you increase your running speed.

**1** USE GOOD FORM: Proper running form will help you achieve your best speed. Bend your arms at a 90-degree angle. and keep your hands open and relaxed. While running. lean forward slightly to keep your momentum going.

**2** PUMP YOUR ARMS: While sprinting. pump your arms straight up and down. Don't swing them across your body.

**3** STAY RELAXED: Focus on relaxing your jaw. shoulders. and hands to keep them from getting tense.

**4** PRACTICE YOUR BURST: Kneel down on one knee with your other foot in front of you. Push off with your foot to burst into a 15-yard (13.7-m) sprint. Do this three times. Then switch your feet and repeat the process.

# NAIL A
# THREE-POINT SHOT

EXTEND SHOOTING ARM
TOWARD BASKET

FLICK WRIST DOWN TO
FOLLOW THROUGH

Your team is down by two points with only seconds left on the clock. If you practice the following tips, you can be a hero by nailing a last-second three-pointer.

**1** It's hard to shoot the ball well if you're wobbly. Line up your body with the basket, and then practice keeping your balance by standing on one foot.

**2** Cradle the ball with your fingertips, not your palm. Support the side of the ball with your non-shooting hand. Focus your eyes on the square above the rim on the backboard.

**3** Bend your knees slightly, and then straighten them as you jump and shoot. Your shooting power comes from your legs, not your arms.

**4** Extend your shooting arm and hand fully when shooting the ball. As you release the ball, follow through by flicking your wrist down. It should look like you're reaching for the rim with your hand.

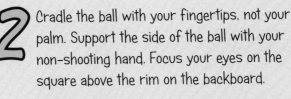

# AWESOME SPORTS DYNASTIES ----------

## BASEBALL

### NEW YORK YANKEES

FOUNDED: in 1901 as an original member of the American League

WINNER OF: a record 27 World Series championship titles

WON: 10 championships between 1947 and 1962

FAMOUS PLAYERS: Babe Ruth, Lou Gehrig, Joe DiMaggio, Mickey Mantle, Yogi Berra, and Derek Jeter

MAJOR LEAGUE BASEBALL HALL OF FAME: includes 44 Yankees players and 11 managers, more than any other team

TEAM VALUE: more than $2 billion

## HOCKEY

### MONTREAL CANADIENS

FOUNDED: in 1909, it is the National Hockey League's (NHL) oldest team

WINNER OF: 24 championships, more than any other NHL team

WON: the Stanley Cup five years in a row from 1956 to 1960, the longest streak in NHL history

FAMOUS PLAYERS: Howie Morenz, Guy Lafleur, Larry Robinson, Jacques Plante, Doug Harvey, Jean Beliveau, Maurice Richard

TEAM VALUE: $575 million

Some fans love them. Other fans hate them. Few things stir up fans' passions more than debating sports dynasties. The following teams have a long history of success. Share these team facts and stats with your friends. Then ask them which team they think should be called the greatest dynasty of all time.

# SOCCER

## MANCHESTER UNITED

**FOUNDED:** in 1878

**WINNER OF:** 20 championship titles and 11 Football Association Challenge Cups (FA Cup)

**WON:** 13 Premier League titles between 1993 and 2013

In the 1998–99 season, won the Premier League, the FA Cup, and the Union of European Football Associations (UEFA) Champions League in one season

**FAMOUS PLAYERS:** Cristiano Ronaldo, Teddy Sheringham, Duncan Edwards, Denis Law, Eric Cantona, Bobby Charlton, George Best

**TEAM VALUE:** more than $3 billion

# TOP TEAMS

| TEAM | CHAMPIONSHIPS |
| --- | --- |
| NEW YORK YANKEES | 27 |
| MONTREAL CANADIENS | 24 |
| MANCHESTER UNITED | 20 |
| BOSTON CELTICS | 17 |
| LOS ANGELES LAKERS | 16 |
| GREEN BAY PACKERS | 13 |
| TORONTO MAPLE LEAFS | 13 |
| DETROIT RED WINGS | 11 |
| ST. LOUIS CARDINALS | 10 |
| CHICAGO BEARS | 9 |
| OAKLAND ATHLETICS | 9 |

■ BASEBALL ■ HOCKEY ■ SOCCER
■ BASKETBALL ■ FOOTBALL

# PULL OFF THE HOOK-AND-LADDER

If you're losing a football game, you may need to try a trick play to get back in it. The hook-and-ladder may provide the spark the offense needs. Keep practicing until you get the timing down, and your opponents will never see it coming!

**1.** Two wide receivers line up next to each other on one side of the field.

**2.** The inside receiver runs faster and a little ahead of the outside receiver. At a set distance he turns, or "hooks," toward the inside of the field.

**3.** The quarterback throws to the inside receiver just as he breaks into his hook.

**4.** After catching the ball, the receiver immediately laterals the ball to the outside receiver behind him. With the right timing, the second receiver can streak toward the end zone without missing a step.

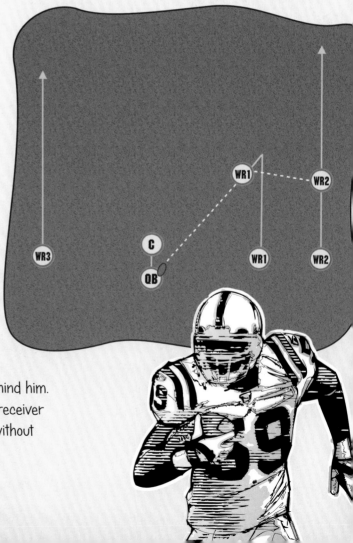

# BLAST A PING-PONG SERVE

In Ping-Pong, getting a good serve is an important part of the game. Here's how to put some spin on your serve to blast it past your opponent.

**Topspin causes the ball to quickly shoot forward when it hits the opponent's side of the table.**

**1.** Hold the paddle at a 45-degree angle facing downward. Start your swing below the ball.

**2.** Swing the paddle upward and away from you to give the ball forward spin.

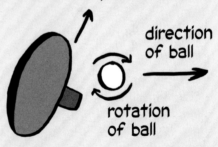

direction of paddle

direction of ball

rotation of ball

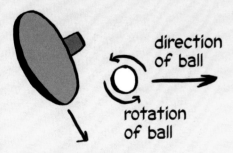

direction of ball

rotation of ball

direction of paddle

**Backspin makes the ball slow down and drop sooner than your opponent expects it to.**

**1.** Hold the paddle at a 45-degree angle facing upward. Start your swing from above the ball.

**2.** Hit the ball with an angled. downward swing to give the ball backward spin.

# AN AWESOME ANCIENT STADIUM

## THE COLOSSEUM

The ancient Romans enjoyed sports as much as we do today. But one sport was very different. In the gladiator games, warriors fought for their lives in gruesome, bloody battles. These men and women were usually prisoners of war and criminals. Their punishment was to fight to the death to entertain huge crowds.

Early gladiator games were often held in fenced fields and public squares. But none of these allowed many people to see the action. Soon the Romans invented the amphitheater—a circular stadium with tiered seating. This new design allowed fans a much better view of the action.

The Colosseum was opened in AD 80. It was the largest and most spectacular stadium of its time. It could seat up to 50,000 bloodthirsty fans, and every floor had bathrooms with running water. Fans could enjoy a variety

of food and drinks and even buy souvenirs. Sometimes a play was performed between events, much like halftime entertainment at today's stadiums. Check out the chart below to see how the Roman Colosseum compares to today's AT&T Stadium near Dallas, Texas.

| | THE COLOSSEUM | AT&T STADIUM |
|---|---|---|
| YEAR OPENED | 80 | 2009 |
| SIZE | 615 feet (187 m) long, 156 feet (47.5 m) high | 900 feet (274 m) long, 800 feet (244 m) high |
| CAPACITY | 50,000 | 80,000; standing room for another 25,000 |
| ROOF | A huge awning could be pulled across the seating area using pulleys and ropes. | A 14,000-ton (12,700-metric ton) retractable steel roof opens and closes in 18 minutes using electric motors. |
| SPECIAL FEATURE | A complex set of underground passages, cages, and rooms was under the arena where gladiators and animals waited to fight. The fighters and animals were sometimes lifted through trap doors in the arena floor for their matches. | A 600-ton (544-metric ton), four-sided video board hangs from the stadium ceiling. Each side features a 162-foot (49-m) wide, high-definition screen. |

# MAKE CITY LIFE MORE AWESOME!

Your bus stops with a mechanical sigh. When you step onto the busy street, you hear honking car horns and thumping stereos. Maybe you smell hot dogs, popcorn, or Chinese food from nearby food carts. What do you want to do? You can go see the newest movie or check out a cool book store. You could also visit a museum, hang out at a beautiful park, and much more. Your options are wide open—this is a busy city!

Chances are good that you live in a city. More than half of the world's population does. Whether you're from a big city, or just plan to visit one, the following tips and suggestions can help make city life more awesome. You'll learn fun games to play, cool places to visit, and how to learn more about a city's history. As you read, remember—cities aren't just places to live. They're also full of awesome experiences!

# PLAY FUN CITY GAMES

Many sports need a lot of open space, which isn't always available in the city. But some sports can be played in smaller spaces such as front yards or school playgrounds. Gather your friends and have some fun trying out the following neighborhood games.

## CAPTURE THE FLAG

You can play this action-packed game across yards or in an alley. You need two teams, each with its own territory. Each team hides a flag or treasure in its territory. Players cross into their opponents' area to try to find the flag and take it safely to their own side. When on the opponents' side, you can be tagged and sent to their "jail" at the back of their territory. Players can rescue jailed teammates by tagging them. The first team to carry the opposing team's flag to their own side wins.

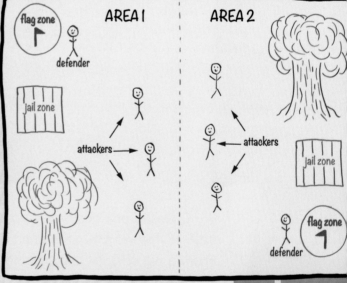

**TIP:** Capture the flag is perfect for neighborhoods with lots of hiding places like trees, bushes, fences, or small sheds. Before you start, create a game plan with your team. Decide who will distract the other team, who will go after the opposing flag, and who will stay to defend your team's flag.

# KICK THE CAN

Guys have been playing this city classic for generations. Maybe your father or grandfather played it! Kick the can is similar to hide-and-seek. You'll need a metal can and at least four players.

1. Find an open area to play and set aside some space for a "jail." Set boundaries so players don't just run to the next block. Then decide which player will be "It."

2. The "It" player places the can in the center of the play area. He then counts out loud to 100 while the other players hide.

3. After counting, the "It" player looks for the hiders. If one is found, he points to the hider and calls out his name. Then both players race back to the can.

4. If "It" gets to the can first, the hider goes to jail. But if the hider gets there first, he kicks the can hard and calls out, "All ye, all ye, out and free!" Anyone in jail is then set free and runs to hide again. The "It" player then has to pick up the can and place it back in the center.

5. If the "It" player sends everyone to jail, the first hider who was caught becomes the new "It" player.

# GO ON A PHOTO SCAVENGER HUNT

Cities are loaded with cool sights to see. Why not gather some buddies and explore your city by going on a photo scavenger hunt? Each person gets a digital camera and a list of items to photograph. Then set a time limit and start taking pictures. You can work alone or in teams of two or three. Whoever gets the most photos on the list wins. Here are some suggestions to get you started:

**A STATUE**

**AN ELECTRIC SIGN**

**A FOUNTAIN**

**SOMETHING THAT HAS BEEN SPILLED**

**A CAR WITH A VANITY LICENSE PLATE**

**A TEAMMATE CLIMBING A TREE**

**A SIDEWALK SIGNBOARD**

**A FLOWERING PLANT**

MANCIPATION

# TIP:

You can make your scavenger hunt "green" by collecting trash as you go. Players can get bonus points for picking up plastic bottles, foam cups, or other trash.

**A POLICE CAR OR FIRE TRUCK**

**A BUILDING WITH STONE COLUMNS**

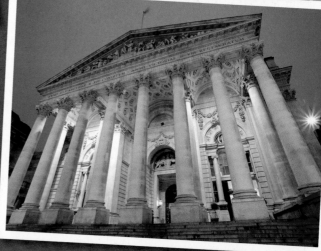

**A CONSTRUCTION SITE**

**A TICKET BOOTH AT A SPORTS STADIUM OR THEATER**

**YOURSELF REFLECTED IN A MIRROR**

**A BIRD NEST ON A BUILDING**

# AWESOME WAYS TO GET AROUND IN CITIES

Many people get around cities in cars or buses. But some cities offer other cool forms of transportation. If you're in a big city, try out one of the following ways to get from place to place.

## SUBWAYS

People in cars often get stuck in traffic jams. But subways can zoom along nonstop powered by up to 625 volts of electricity! London had the world's first underground railway, which opened in 1863. Although its nickname is "the Tube," more than half of the Underground's tracks are actually above ground.

The New York City subway is another famous system. When it opened in 1904, it had 9 miles (14.5 kilometers) of track. Today New York's subway system has 660 miles (1,062 km) of track and carries 5.4 million riders each weekday.

## PUBLIC BIKES

Many cities have a system for renting or sharing bicycles. Bike stations are set up throughout the city. People check out a bike at one station, ride it where they need to go, and then check it in at another station. China has the world's largest bike sharing program, called the Hangzhou Public Bicycle Program. Several other cities have similar programs, including the Vélib' system in Paris, France, CitiRide in New York, and Nice Ride in Minneapolis, Minnesota.

# AWESOME TRAVEL BETWEEN CITIES

There are some awesome ways people can travel from one city to another as well. Here are a couple incredible ways people travel between cities and countries in some parts of the world.

## THE SHINKANSEN

The Shinkansen inter-city rail line in Japan is nicknamed the "Bullet Train." It moves people between Japan's two main islands at speeds up to 200 miles (322 km) per hour! It is one of the busiest rail lines in the world. The Shinkansen carries more than 150 million passengers every year.

## THE CHUNNEL

In Europe the Channel Tunnel, or "Chunnel," goes under the English Channel to connect England and France. It travels about 24 miles (38.6 km) underwater, which makes it the longest underwater tunnel in the world. The Chunnel is used by both passenger trains and freight trains. Some people even drive their cars onto a train car to catch a ride between the two countries.

# WILD ANIMALS IN THE CITY

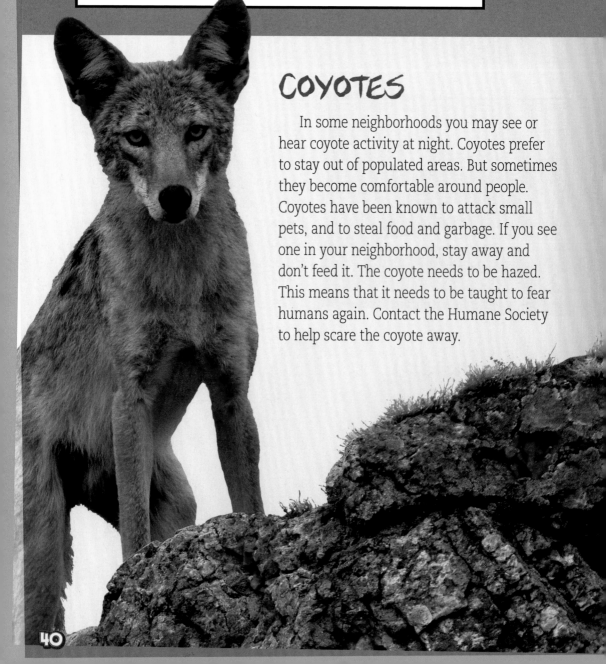

## COYOTES

In some neighborhoods you may see or hear coyote activity at night. Coyotes prefer to stay out of populated areas. But sometimes they become comfortable around people. Coyotes have been known to attack small pets, and to steal food and garbage. If you see one in your neighborhood, stay away and don't feed it. The coyote needs to be hazed. This means that it needs to be taught to fear humans again. Contact the Humane Society to help scare the coyote away.

Have you ever taken out the trash and discovered a fat raccoon or opossum sitting on the dumpster? When we think of wild animals, we don't normally think of the city. But cities do have some wildlife living in them. Read on to learn what you should do if you come across a wild animal in your neighborhood.

# WILD DOGS

Most stray dogs in the city aren't truly wild animals. But you still need to be careful if you see one. If the dog is scared or sick, it can be dangerous. Take note of its behavior. If the dog is baring its teeth, growling, and acting aggressive—stay away. Call your local animal control service so officials can safely move it.

However, if the dog seems happy and friendly, you can try to return it to its owner. If it's wearing a collar and tags, check for an address and phone number. Call the owners and let them know you found their pet. If there is no collar, take the dog to an animal control service. Officers there may be able to find the dog's owners, or help find a good home for it.

# ALLIGATORS

Have you heard stories about alligators living in city sewers? Actually, such stories are just popular myths. Alligators are tropical animals. It's too cold in most city sewers for them. But occasionally alligators are seen roaming the streets in cities with warm climates. They can also show up in parks near swampy areas where they live.

If you happen to see one of these powerful reptiles, back away quickly. Try to stay at least 15 feet (4.6 meters) away. Alligators can't run fast for long. But they can cover short distances very quickly. Call animal control so the animal can be moved to a safe location.

If an alligator does manage to get you in its jaws, you need to fight back as hard as you can. The animal will probably try to drag you into nearby water, where you would drown. Hit or poke the alligator in the eyes with something hard. If you can't get at the eyes, go for its nostrils.

# RACCOONS AND OPOSSUMS

These animals can live just about anywhere—even in a busy city. They might make their homes in people's garages, attics, or sheds. And they'll eat just about anything, including garbage. Sometimes these animals seem cute, but they can carry disease. Plus, they can be nasty fighters.

To keep them away, don't let them smell food or trash. Get a trashcan with a sealable lid. Keep pet food inside and put away any leftovers. If you see one of these animals coming toward you, back away—especially if they have food or young nearby. They normally don't want anything to do with humans. If you leave them alone, they'll usually leave you alone. But if you see one that continues to cause problems, call your local animal control office to get rid of it.

## MIGHTY RAPTORS

Many birds of prey nest in the nooks and window ledges of tall city buildings. Look up and you might see raptors circling high above the streets. If you're lucky, you might see a peregrine falcon diving at speeds up to 200 miles (322 km) per hour to snatch its prey! One family of peregrine falcons has nested at Legg Mason tower in Baltimore, Maryland, for many generations. Search the Internet for raptor Webcams, and you can watch these awesome birds in their urban nests.

# GROW A COOL INDOOR PLANT

You don't need to live in the country or have a big garden to grow some cool plants. Plants help add personality to any home, no matter where you live. Here are several interesting plants you can grow in an apartment or other small indoor space.

cactus

**CACTUS** Some types of cactus are very colorful, and they hardly need any maintenance.

glow-in-the-dark mushrooms

**ALOE VERA** This plant is easy to grow and cool to look at. Its sap also has healing properties. People often use it to soothe burns.

**MUSHROOMS** Some edible mushrooms are tasty and loaded with nutrients. Others are poisonous and shouldn't be eaten, but all are weird and interesting to look at. Some even glow in the dark! Get some moist soil and a clear bowl or tank. Set it up in a cool dark place and see if you can grow your own glow-in-the-dark fungus!

# DWARF FRUIT TREE

You can grow your own fruit right in your living room! Dwarf fruit trees grow only a few feet tall and are easy to care for. Try growing your own apples, oranges, bananas, cherries, or other delicious fruit.

# VENUS FLYTRAP

What a cool plant. It not only brings greenery into your home—it also catches and eats bugs!

Venus flytrap

BURP!

dwarf fruit tree

# COMMUNITY GARDENS

In cities with little green space, people sometimes work together to grow community gardens. As people grow fruits and vegetables, they often grow closer as a community. People help make their neighborhoods nicer to look at and often become good friends as well. Do an Internet search to see if any community gardens are in your area. If not, maybe you can start one with your neighbors.

# VISIT AWESOME CITY BUILDINGS

Cities everywhere have cool or unusual architecture. Take a look around where you live. You might find a funky bridge, a massive old flourmill, or some other weird building. Ask a librarian to help you learn about unique structures where you live. Then go see them in person. Here are some examples of awesome buildings in cities around the world.

## THE FOREST SPIRAL

This housing complex in Darmstadt, Germany, opened in 2000. The building rises up in a spiral pattern. Its diagonal roof is covered with grass, trees, and other plants.

## KANSAS CITY PUBLIC LIBRARY

The Kansas City Public Library in Kansas City, Missouri, looks just like a library shelf lined with giant books. Even the interior is designed to look like you are entering a huge book.

## GUGGENHEIM MUSEUM

The Guggenheim Museum in Bilbao, Spain, opened in 1997. The art museum's design features a unique combination of shapes. The building itself is like a work of art.

## SYDNEY OPERA HOUSE

The Sydney Opera House opened in 1973 in New South Wales, Australia. It sits on a point of land in Sydney Harbour and is surrounded by water on three sides. With its curved shell roof design, it resembles a large sailing ship sitting on the water.

# PLAY COOL NEIGHBORHOOD SPORTS

## DISC GOLF

You can play this game alone, but it's more fun with a few friends. Each player needs a flying disc, such as a Frisbee. Choose a starting point, such as someone's front steps. Then choose your first target, or "hole," to hit with the discs. The target can be a tree trunk, bike rack, tire swing, or anything else that won't be damaged easily.

Each player takes a turn at the starting point throwing his disc toward the target. The players then find their discs and keep taking turns until they each hit the target. Keep track of each player's strokes as you play. Then pick a new target and repeat the process. A full game includes nine holes. At the end of the ninth hole, the player with the lowest score wins.

# STOOPBALL

This is another classic game that's perfect for guys who want to play baseball but don't have much space. You'll need a quiet side street with little to no traffic. You'll also need two teams of two or three players, a tennis ball or other bouncy rubber ball, and a stoop.

**1.** One player begins as the batter. The player stands in the street by the curb and faces the stoop. His teammates and the other team spread out behind him.

**2.** The batter starts by throwing the ball hard against the stoop. The goal is to bounce the ball back onto the street as many times as possible. If the ball bounces on the sidewalk, it's a strike. After three strikes, the batter is out.

**3.** If the ball bounces in the street once, it's a single. An imaginary runner, called a ghost runner, goes to first base. If the ball bounces twice, it's a double and ghost runners advance two bases. Three bounces are a triple and four bounces count as a home run. Every time a ghost runner gets to home plate, the batting team scores a point.

**4.** If a player on the other team catches the ball before it bounces in the street, it's an out. After three outs, the teams switch sides.

**TIP:** Use neighborhood objects such as mailboxes or benches to set foul lines for the game.

# AWESOME FREE THINGS TO DO IN A CITY

Are you short on cash? No worries! One of the great things about cities is that there are tons of awesome free things to do. Try out the following ideas, and then take a look around your city. You'll probably find hundreds of other cool free things you can do.

1. **TOUR HISTORICAL SITES.** Every city has its own unique history. Ask your librarian to help you learn about the history in your city. Then visit the places where important events have happened.

2. **TOUR CITY SERVICES.** Your city probably has water treatment plants, public transportation centers, and other places that the public can tour. It's a great way to learn how your city works.

3. **VISIT A LIBRARY.** The world is at your fingertips at the library. From classic books to the Internet, libraries are great places to let your imagination soar.

4. **VISIT A MUSEUM.** Most cities have museums or art galleries filled with incredible artifacts and artwork. Some of these places are completely free. Many others have certain days that are free and open to the public.

5. **GO TO A PARK.** You may not have a big backyard, but most cities do an awesome job of creating parks and other public outdoor spaces. Nature is also good for your mood—and your brain! Studies show that spending time in nature increases your ability to focus.

3

4

5

6

7

9

6. **VOLUNTEER TO HELP.** There are dozens of ways you can help in your community. You can help clean up a park or other public space. You can offer to help do chores for the elderly. Or you can ask how you can help at a local charity or an animal shelter.

7. **GO GEOCACHING.** People often think this outdoor treasure-hunting game is only done in the wilderness. But it can take place in cities too. Do some research online about geocaching in your area. You can use a Global Positioning System (GPS) device if you have one. Or just print out a map and follow clues to find treasures hidden near you.

8. **VISIT PUBLIC ART AND ART FESTIVALS.** Many cities have a variety of public statues, sculptures, and artwork that anyone can go see. Search your city's website to learn where they are located. You can also check out any free art festivals that may be held in your city.

9. **WALK OR BIKE.** Learn about your city while getting some exercise at the same time. Cities often feature interesting hiking and biking trails, and some cities offer awesome walking tours.

# CITY FESTIVALS

Many large cities hold festivals that are an important part of their history and culture. For example, Carnival takes place every year in Rio de Janeiro, Brazil. And New Orleans, Louisiana, is well known for its Mardi Gras festival. At these celebrations thousands of people enjoy parades, lively music, colorful costumes, and a lot of delicious food.

Carnival parade in Rio de Janeiro

# WHICH CITY WAS SCARIEST?

Throughout history, life in big cities has often been gross and dangerous.

Even modern cities can have their share of disease and pollution. Which of these historical cities would you be the most scared to live in?

ANCIENT ROME

MEDIEVAL LONDON

|  | ANCIENT ROME | MEDIEVAL LONDON |
|---|---|---|
| CRIME | Ancient Rome was a dangerous place. The city couldn't afford police officers. Thieves and violent gangs roamed the streets at all hours. | During the Middle Ages (about 400-1500), violent crime was common. Criminals often went unpunished. But if they were caught, punishment was severe. The bodies of hanged criminals were often left on display for weeks as a warning to other lawbreakers. |
| HEALTH | Most Roman people were slaves or very poor. They usually lived in crowded, filthy apartments. Their food was often filled with parasites. People suffered from terrible diseases, such as malaria and typhoid. Even worse, both sick and healthy people commonly bathed together in public baths, which just helped spread disease. | People didn't know about germs hundreds of years ago. Many thought disease spread through bad smells or bad luck. In the mid-1300s, bubonic plague killed tens of millions of people worldwide. So many died that the dead had to be buried in mass graves. |
| GROSS FACT | Instead of using bathrooms, poor Romans relieved themselves in chamber pots. In the morning they would dump the pots out the window into the street. Look out below! | Many doctors thought sicknesses came from evil spirits. They sometimes cut holes in patients' skulls to let the bad spirits "bleed out." Not surprisingly, few patients survived this "cure." |

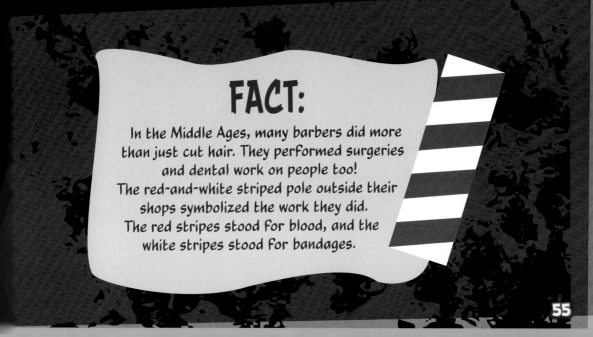

# FACT:

In the Middle Ages, many barbers did more than just cut hair. They performed surgeries and dental work on people too!
The red-and-white striped pole outside their shops symbolized the work they did.
The red stripes stood for blood, and the white stripes stood for bandages.

# INCREDIBLE CITY RECORDS

## FIRST CHEESEBURGER

**PASADENA,** California, was home to Lionel Sternberger. In 1924 he reportedly became the first person to slap a slice of cheese on a burger. Thanks for the awesome sandwich, Lionel!

## LARGEST POPULATION

When comparing individual cities, **SHANGHAI,** China, easily has the biggest population in the world. Nearly 18 million people live inside Shanghai's city limits. However, look beyond the main city to include the suburbs, and Shanghai drops out of the top 10. The city with the largest metro area population is **TOKYO,** Japan, with about 32 million people.

## MOST SPORTS CHAMPIONSHIPS

**NEW YORK CITY** boasts the most sports championships of any city in the world. The city's baseball, basketball, football, and hockey teams have claimed a total of 55 championship titles.

## BIGGEST ROCK STARS

**LIVERPOOL,** England, was home to the Beatles. The Beatles have sold more albums than any other band in history.

## MOST U.S. PRESIDENTS

The **CHARLOTTESVILLE**, Virginia, area has supplied the most U.S. presidents. Thomas Jefferson, James Madison, and James Monroe were all born in or near Charlottesville.

## TALLEST BUILDING

The city of **DUBAI**, United Arab Emirates, claims the world's tallest building. The Burj Khalifa skyscraper opened in January 2010 and is 2,722 feet (830 meters) tall. That's more than half a mile high!

## MOST AMUSEMENT PARK VISITORS

**LAKE BUENA VISTA**, Florida, has only 10 permanent residents. However, it is home to Disney World's Magic Kingdom theme park and Typhoon Lagoon water park. Nearly 17.5 million people visit the Magic Kingdom each year, and more than 2 million people visit Typhoon Lagoon.

## MOST MULTI-MILLIONAIRES

**LONDON**, England, is home to 4,224 multi-millionaires. The city also hosts the second most tourists in the world. Almost 17 million people visited London in 2012.

# MAKE THE OUTDOORS MORE AWESOME!

Have you ever dreamed of going on an outdoor adventure? Out in the wild, you can slash your way through the underbrush while finding your way by the stars. You can forage for food and water using nothing but your wits. If you encounter a wild animal, you can stare it down and have a great story to share with your friends.

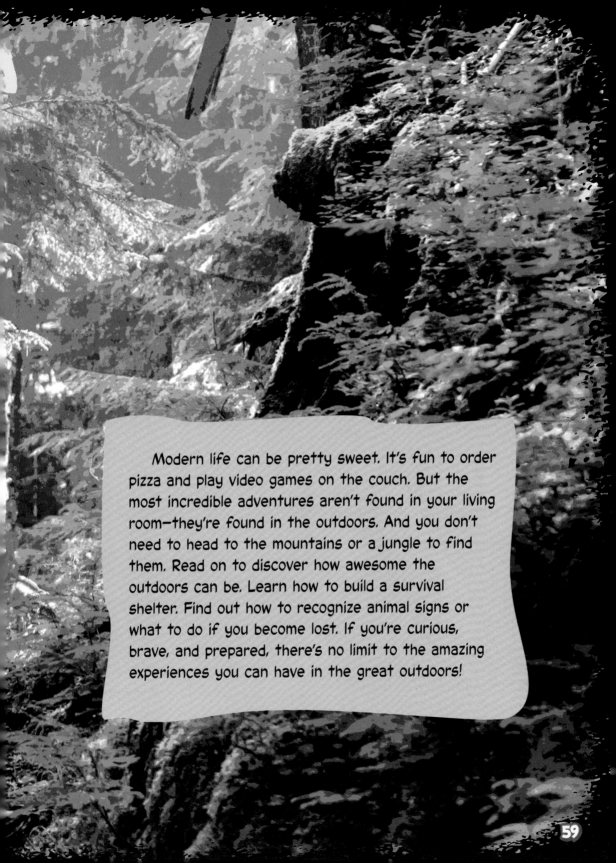

Modern life can be pretty sweet. It's fun to order pizza and play video games on the couch. But the most incredible adventures aren't found in your living room—they're found in the outdoors. And you don't need to head to the mountains or a jungle to find them. Read on to discover how awesome the outdoors can be. Learn how to build a survival shelter. Find out how to recognize animal signs or what to do if you become lost. If you're curious, brave, and prepared, there's no limit to the amazing experiences you can have in the great outdoors!

# MAKE HIKES FUN

Hiking is a great, fun way to experience the outdoors. Hiking costs very little, and it can be an awesome adventure if you plan ahead. Going with a couple of friends can make your hike safer and a lot more fun. Bring along a cell phone in case of an emergency. And stay on marked trails to avoid getting lost—which wouldn't be much fun at all.

# TIPS FOR A GREAT HIKE

1. Research the area and trails before you go. Set goals for what you want to see, and take note of possible dangers to avoid.

2. Make up a story about the area as you go. Let people in your group make up different parts of the story.

3. Make your hike into a scavenger hunt. Look for items like colorful flowers, animal tracks, or unusual rocks. Bring along a camera to take photos of the items on your list.

4. Wear layers of clothes. If it gets too hot you can simply take off a layer. If it gets colder, you can put it back on.

5. Pack wisely. Bring along a compass, map, camping knife, lighter or waterproof matches, bug spray, water, and food.

6. Take a break. Breaks help you conserve your energy, and it gives you a chance to take in the natural surroundings.

# FIND YOUR WAY IF YOU'RE LOST

When adventuring in the wild, a compass can help you find your way. If you get lost without one, don't panic. Just use these easy methods to help you navigate to safety.

## USE A STICK

On a sunny day, place a 3-foot (0.9-meter) stick straight up and down in the ground. Place a small rock at the tip of the stick's shadow. Wait about 15 minutes and place another rock at the shadow's tip again. Next, draw a line between the two rocks.

The first rock you placed represents west, and the second is east. The line between them points exactly east and west. Draw another straight line across the middle of the first. This line will point north and south.

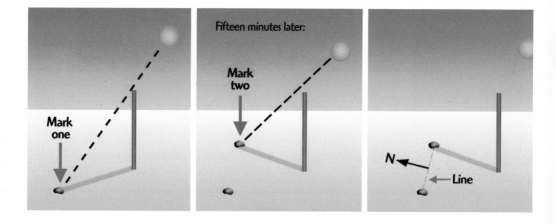

Mark one

Fifteen minutes later:

Mark two

N ← Line

# USE A WATCH

You can find north and south using an analog (non-digital) watch. Point the hour hand directly toward the sun. Then draw an imaginary line midway between the hour hand and 12:00 on the watch. This line will point directly south. The opposite direction is north.

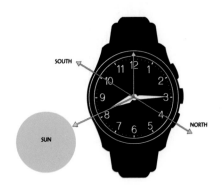

# USE THE STARS

In the northern hemisphere, find the Big Dipper. Follow an imaginary line from the two stars at the front of the Big Dipper to a bright star a short distance away. This is the North Star, which is also the end of the handle of the Little Dipper. Look straight down from the North Star to the ground and you will be facing north.

In the southern hemisphere, find the Southern Cross constellation. Imagine a straight line extending out from the bottom of the cross. Below the cross are two bright stars. Imagine a second line extending from a point between the two stars. Note the point where the two lines meet. Look directly down from this point to the ground to find south.

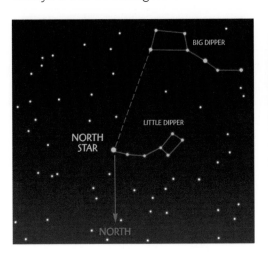

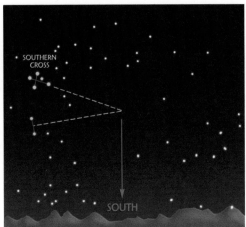

# FIND WATER IN THE WILD

Getting lost in the wilderness can be a cold, lonely, and scary experience. If this happens to you, it's important to stay calm. Take a deep breath and get hold of your fear. The next thing you need to do is find water—you won't last long without it. People can live only a few days without water. Here are three ways to find water in the wild. They can be fun to practice—even if your life is not in danger.

## Collect Rainwater

Use a cup or bowl if you have it. If not, create a rain trap. Lay a plastic bag or rain jacket over a hole in the ground to form a crude bowl. Place rocks on the outer edges to hold the plastic in place.

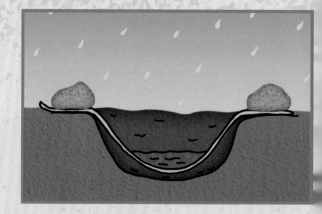

## Collect Dew

Dew forms overnight as air temperatures cool. You can use a rain trap to collect the dew. Or you can soak it up from a grassy area with an absorbent cloth. Then just squeeze the water into a container.

# Collect Condensation

Find a tree or plant with large leaves in a sunny area. Place a clear plastic bag over the leaves, and then tie the bag shut. Water will evaporate from the leaves and condense inside the bag. When there's enough water, simply remove the bag and drink the water or pour it into a container.

# REMEMBER THE RULES OF THREE

**THREE MINUTES:** about how long you can survive without oxygen

**THREE HOURS:** about how long you can survive without shelter in extremely hot or cold temperatures

**THREE DAYS:** about how long you can survive without water

**THREE WEEKS:** about how long you can survive without food

 If you get lost, you might get hungry. But food should be the last of your worries! Water and shelter should be your first concern.

# EAT SOME PLANTS

If you're lost in the wild, you'll eventually need to eat. You'll improve your chances if you know about wildcrafting, or looking for food in the wild. But you need to be careful. Some berries and parts of plants might look tasty. But they could be poisonous. They may make you sick or even kill you. Generally, you should avoid plants that:

- **STINK**

- **ARE BRIGHTLY COLORED**

- **HAVE SPINES, FINE HAIR, OR THORNS**

These are nature's way of telling you to stay away. Don't eat any plant if you don't know what it is. If you plan to go exploring, get a guidebook to plants of the area ahead of time. Then if you get lost, you'll have clear information on what you can and cannot eat.

| EDIBLE PLANTS | NON-EDIBLE PLANTS |
|---|---|
| Edible Berries (blackberries, raspberries, strawberries, blueberries) | Poisonous Berries (baneberry, belladonna, elderberry, nightshade, Jerusalem cherry) |
| Edible Nuts (hickory nuts, acorns, pine nuts, beech nuts) | Poisonous Nuts (buckeye nuts, physic nuts) |
| Wild Rice | Rosary Peas |
| Cattail Roots | Hemlock |
| Prickly Pear Cactus | Most Mushrooms |

# EAT SOME BUGS

It may sound gross, but you can eat many kinds of bugs and worms. Bugs have a lot of protein that can help keep you alive. Worms are usually found in cool, moist soil. Many bugs, such as ants, termites, or grubs can often be found under the bark of dead trees.

Like with plants, avoid bugs that are brightly colored or hairy, since they are likely poisonous. You also should avoid bugs that sting or bite, such as mosquitoes and bees, which could carry disease. You can eat some bugs raw. But if you can get a fire going, it's best to cook them first. Cooked bugs are safer to eat and are usually better tasting.

| EDIBLE BUGS | NON-EDIBLE BUGS |
| --- | --- |
| 1. Crickets | 1. Fireflies |
| 2. Grubs | 2. Hairy or Spiky Caterpillars |
| 3. Grasshoppers/Locusts | 3. Blister Beetles |
| 4. Termites and Ants | 4. Flies |
| 5. Earthworms | 5. Ticks |

# TRUE ADVENTURE STORIES – PART I

An awesome trek into the wilderness is great, but there's rarely much risk involved. Even if you get lost, Global Positioning System (GPS) devices and cell phones can usually help you find your way. Sometimes you have to go out of your way to find true adventure. Here are a couple of stories about guys who created their own awesome life adventures.

## THE ADVENTURE OF A LIFETIME

American Jeffrey Tayler felt like he needed a change in his life. Feeling the need for adventure, he quit his job and flew to Africa in 1995. There he bought a hand-carved canoe called a pirogue. With the help of just one African guide, Tayler paddled more than 1,000 miles (1,609 km) down the Congo River. Along the way he faced dangerous wild animals, scorching heat, powerful storms, and millions of biting insects.

In spite of the difficulties, Tayler said it was the greatest adventure of his life. He later wrote a book about his experiences called *Facing the Congo*.

# SAILING SOLO

In 1999 Australian Jesse Martin finished an adventure that he began nearly a year before. He sailed all the way around the world in a 34-foot (10-meter) boat—by himself! During his journey he survived several severe storms, extreme temperatures, and terrible loneliness. That alone makes his story incredible. But he also set a record with his adventure. At just 18 years old, he became the youngest person to ever sail around the world alone.

Jesse recorded his journey with a video camera mounted on the boat. The footage was later used in a movie about his adventure called *Lionheart: The Jesse Martin Story.* Jesse's voyage took 328 days and covered more than 27,000 nautical miles (50,000 km).

# FIND EVIDENCE OF WILD ANIMALS

It can be difficult to spot wild animals. They usually stay hidden from humans. But you can learn which animals live in an area by observing the clues they leave behind. Look for their tracks in fresh snow, mud, or dirt. Watch for wild animal scat, or poop, that they leave in the woods. Some animals mark trees by chewing, scratching, or pecking on their trunks. And if you look closely, you may even spot their dens and nests while hiking in the wild.

## SOME WILD ANIMAL SCAT:

Bear

Deer

Fox

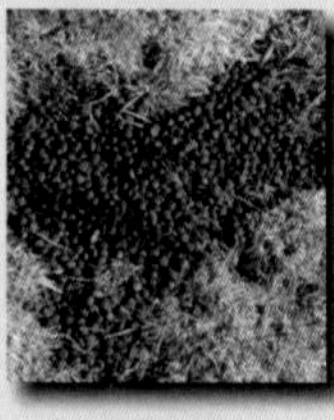

Hare

Lynx

Moose

Raccoon

Wolf

Beaver

# SOME ANIMALS AND THEIR TRACKS:

Deer

Mouse

Brown Bear

Hare

Beaver

Turkey

Fox

Hedgehog

Wolf

Badger

Lynx

Raccoon

Moose

Wild Boar

# SURVIVE WILD ANIMAL ATTACKS — PART I

It's a wild world out there, but try to stay calm. Wild animal attacks are very rare. It's best to avoid dangerous animals in the wild. But if you do see one, keep your distance. Wild animals usually won't attack unless they feel threatened.

There is also safety in numbers, so hiking or camping in groups is a good idea. The following tips can help you to avoid or—if needed—survive an attack.

## BEARS

With immense strength and razor-sharp teeth, bears can be deadly if they attack. Here are some tips for dealing with these powerful creatures if you meet them in the wild:

### CARRY BEAR REPELLENT

These sprays do a good job of keeping bears away.

### BACK AWAY SLOWLY

Don't run. Hold up your arms to make yourself look bigger. Make a lot of noise as you back off slowly.

### USE WHATEVER YOU CAN

If the bear attacks, you'll need to defend yourself any way you can. Use a big rock or stick as a weapon. Go for the bear's sensitive areas, such as its eyes or nose.

# MOUNTAIN LIONS

A mountain lion, or cougar, can be deadly—especially if it feels threatened. If you see one in the wild, don't run! Running will make the cat think you are prey. Follow these tips to survive a mountain lion attack:

## DON'T PLAY DEAD

Acting dead just tells the cat you're helpless. Research shows that even standing still could trigger an attack.

## MAKE YOURSELF LOOK BIGGER

Let the mountain lion know you're not to be messed with. Make loud noises and wave your arms around. Try to make yourself look larger and more threatening.

## FIGHT BACK

If the cat still attacks you, you'll need to fight back. Use whatever weapons you can find, like sticks or rocks. Some people have even managed to fight off cougars with their bare hands.

# AWESOME ATTACK ANIMALS

Wild animals have an amazing variety of attack styles. Here are a couple of the most unique styles found in nature.

## BULLET ANTS

When threatened, these South American ants use powerful stingers to drive off an attacker. People who have been stung by them say it's so painful that it feels like being shot by a bullet.

## ELECTRIC EELS

Zzzzzap! The electric eel can pump out up to 600 volts of electricity to stun its prey silly.

# BUILD A
# SURVIVAL SHELTER

A survival shelter can protect you from rain, cold,
and bugs. It can also provide shade on hot sunny days.
Here's how to build a basic debris hut in the woods.

1. Pick a high spot where rain will flow away from your shelter. If possible, build your shelter near your supplies.

2. Find a straight branch that is 6 to 8 feet (1.8 to 2.4 m) long. This will be the ridgepole for the roof.

3. Prop up one end of the branch on a stump or forked tree. Set the other end on the ground.

4. Find several long, straight sticks. Set them against both sides of the ridgepole to form the ribs of the roof. Leave the high end open to form a doorway.

5. Next, lay several large leafy branches across the ribs to form the roof.

6. Now find a large amount of dry grass or leaves to use as insulation. Put about 2 feet (0.6 meter) of material on top of the roof. Add some more small branches on top to keep the insulation in place.

7. Finally, place more grass or leaves on the floor and in the doorway of the shelter. This will help hold your body heat inside.

# BUILD A BAMBOO FISHING POLE

From advanced rods to electronic fish finders, modern fishing has become high-tech. But who needs fancy gear when you can make your own? Build this easy homemade fishing pole, and soon you'll be bringing in a great catch!

## WHAT YOU'LL NEED:

- Pole: A 5-foot (1.5-m) piece of 3/4-inch (1.9-centimeter) bamboo from a garden shop.

- Line: You can use regular fishing line. But kite string also works well and is a lot cheaper.

- Fish Hooks: Size 6 or 8.

- Bobber: This floating marker helps you see when you've hooked a fish. You can buy a standard bobber at the store. Or you can just attach a piece of cork to your line with a rubber band.

- Sinkers: These weights help your hook and bait sink to where the fish are. Store-bought sinkers are easy to find. But you can also use simple washers or nuts.

1.

2.

1. Wrap one end of the fishing line around one end of the pole and tie it in place. You could also use some duct tape to help hold it in place.

2. Attach your cork or bobber to the line about 2 feet (0.6 m) above the hook.

3. Next, tie a nut or sinker to the line a few inches above where you will tie on the hook.

3.

4. Finally, tie a hook onto the end of the line. Follow the diagram below to tie the hook on using a strong clinch knot. Now you're ready to haul in some fish!

4.

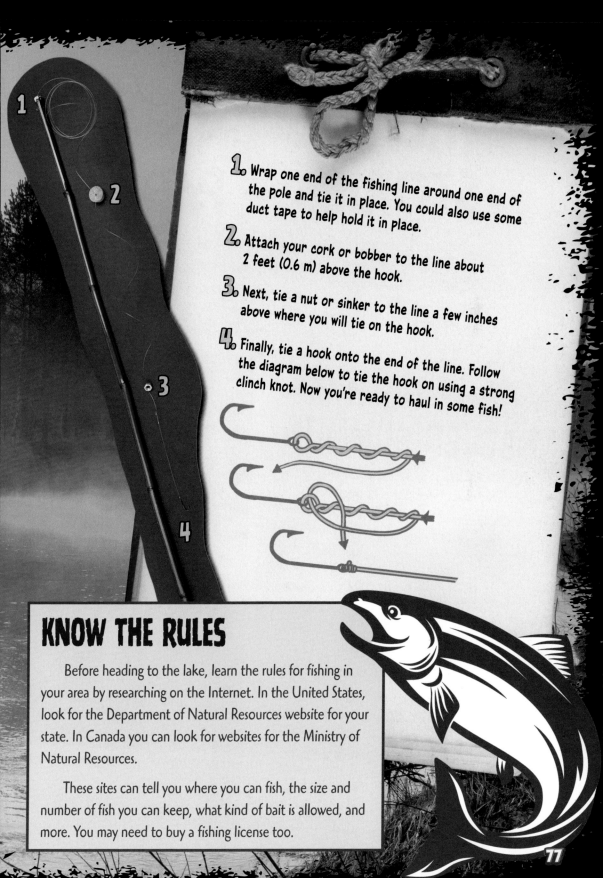

# KNOW THE RULES

Before heading to the lake, learn the rules for fishing in your area by researching on the Internet. In the United States, look for the Department of Natural Resources website for your state. In Canada you can look for websites for the Ministry of Natural Resources.

These sites can tell you where you can fish, the size and number of fish you can keep, what kind of bait is allowed, and more. You may need to buy a fishing license too.

# TRUE ADVENTURE STORIES – PART II

History is filled with stories of men and women who have had incredible adventures. But kids have had some awesome adventures too. Here are a couple kids who could inspire even the hardiest adventurers.

## CLIMBING THE SEVEN SUMMITS

As a boy Jordan Romero made an incredible goal for himself. He decided he would climb the highest mountain on each of the world's seven continents. Known as the "Seven Summits," nobody had climbed all of them at such a young age.

When he was 10 years old, Jordan climbed to the peak of Mt. Kilimanjaro in Africa. At age 13 he climbed the world's highest mountain, Mt. Everest in Tibet. Everest's peak is 29,035 feet (8,850 m) high, and Jordan was the youngest person ever to reach it. When he was 15, Jordan finished his goal by climbing to the peak of Mt. Vinson Massif in Antarctica.

Jordan set a record as the youngest person ever to conquer the Seven Summits. At the top of Vinson Massif, Jordan called his mom from a satellite phone to celebrate his amazing achievement.

# ONE LONG HIKE

What's the longest walk you've ever taken? Omar Castillo Gallegos probably has you beat. It all started in 1985 when he was just 8 years old. Omar saw a TV show about the rain forests being destroyed in Mexico. He didn't like how animals' homes were being destroyed.

Omar wanted the Mexican government to protect the rain forest. So he decided to walk 800 miles (1,287 km) from his home in Mexico City to the rain forest to get the government's attention.

Omar's walk took 39 days and he wore out three pairs of shoes along the way. Omar soon gained a lot of attention. People began joining him for parts of his walk. It became like a parade. News stations began doing stories about him and his mission. In the end, Omar's long walk was worth it. Mexico's president promised to try to do what he could to help preserve Mexico's rain forests.

rain forest destruction in Mexico

# ADVENTUROUS AUTHORS

Some of the world's greatest authors have also been awesome adventurers. Here are three guys who didn't just write amazing adventure stories. They were also tough as nails and great outdoorsmen themselves. Talk about these adventurers with your friends and decide who was the most awesome and adventurous author.

## JACK LONDON

### Books

London wrote more than 40 novels, including *White Fang*, *The Sea Wolf*, and *The Call of the Wild*.

### Jobs

London worked as an oyster pirate, a sailor on a sealing ship, a war journalist, and a gold miner.

### Great adventure

At age 17, he piloted the ship *Sophie Sutherland* through a typhoon off the coast of Japan.

### Awesome quote

*"The more difficult the feat, the greater the satisfaction at its accomplishment."*

# ERNEST HEMINGWAY

## Books

Hemingway wrote 10 novels, including *The Sun Also Rises*, *A Farewell to Arms*, *For Whom the Bell Tolls*, and *The Old Man and the Sea*. He also wrote several collections of short stories.

## Jobs

Hemingway worked as an ambulance driver in World War I (1914–1918), a war journalist, a boxer, a big game hunter, and militia leader in World War II (1939–1945).

## Great adventure

During World War I, Hemingway was severely wounded by mortar fire on July 8, 1918. In spite of his injuries, Hemingway managed to carry a fellow wounded soldier to safety.

## Awesome quote

*"Courage is grace under pressure."*

# SIR ARTHUR CONAN DOYLE

## Books

Doyle wrote more than 25 novels and numerous short stories. But he's best known for his Sherlock Holmes books, including *The Adventures of Sherlock Holmes* and *The Hound of the Baskervilles*.

## Jobs

Doyle worked as a sailor on a whaling ship, a ship's doctor, a body builder, a soccer goalie, and a criminal investigator.

## Great adventure

When he was 20 years old, Doyle worked aboard the whaling ship *Hope* as the ship's surgeon. He often fell into the icy waters of the Arctic Ocean while helping crew members on the ship's deck.

## Awesome quote

*"There are heroisms all round us waiting to be done."*

# SURVIVE WILD ANIMAL ATTACKS – PART II

## RATTLESNAKE

Rattlesnakes can be up to 8 feet (2.4 m) long. They can see in the dark. And they are camouflaged, so they are difficult to see in tall grass or under shrubs. They also have long, sharp fangs that inject deadly venom, and their strike is lightning quick. Follow these tips if you ever find yourself in rattlesnake country.

### AVOID THEM

Know what rattlers look like, and be on the lookout. Don't reach into places where snakes like to hide, such as piles of rocks or sticks. Listen for their warning rattling sound. Wear boots, long pants, and thick socks for protection in case they do try to bite.

### GET AWAY

If you see a snake—freeze. Then back away slowly until you're at least 6 to 8 feet (1.8 to 2.4 m) away. Then run!

### TREAT BITE WOUNDS

Don't try to cut open the wound and suck out the poison. That's just for the movies. Instead, keep the bite below heart level and don't move around too much. Movement makes the poison spread more quickly through your body. Call 911 right away.

# SKUNK

Skunks normally won't attack you. But if they feel threatened, they'll defend themselves with a nasty spray.

## BE COOL

If you see a skunk, don't threaten it. Stand still or walk away.

## KNOW WHEN TO RUN

If the skunk starts to stomp its feet or turns its rear end toward you, run! Skunk spray can cause nausea, coughing, shortness of breath, and even temporary blindness.

## DEODORIZE

If you do get sprayed, you'll need to neutralize it. Mix together 1 quart (0.9 liter) of hydrogen peroxide, 1/4 cup (60 mL) of baking soda, and 1 teaspoon (5 mL) of mild dishwashing soap. Then wash yourself all over with the mixture. You might need to do it more than once.

# ALLIGATORS AND CROCODILES

If you're lost in a swamp and see a 12 foot (3.7 meter) alligator swimming your way—run! Alligators and crocodiles have the most powerful jaws of any living creature. Scientists think a large crocodile's bite force is about the same as the mighty Tyrannosaurus rex once had. If one bites you, you're in serious trouble.

But not all hope is lost. These animals can move only about 10 miles (16 km) per hour for a short distance. If one comes at you, run away at full speed. You should be able to escape.

If running isn't an option, there's another defense you can try. These reptiles' jaws are powerful when biting down, but they are very weak when opening. If necessary, try to get your arms around the animal's snout. You should be able to hold its jaws shut until it gives up—just don't let go!

# MAKE EVERY DAY MORE AWESOME!

When the bell rings at the end of the school day, what do you do? You have no homework and a wide-open afternoon. You could just head home and watch TV. Maybe you could play video games with your friends. Or instead, perhaps you could do something new, challenging, and adventurous!

Every day has opportunities to do awesome things. On the following pages you'll find lots of ideas for making your days more awesome. You'll learn how to make a stop-motion movie, start your own business, study better for tests, and a lot more. Try the suggested ideas or make up your own. Be creative and challenge yourself to make each day as awesome as it can be!

# INVENT A SECRET CODE

You and your friend created an awesome battle plan for an upcoming laser tag match. But a guy from the other team saw your notes, and now he knows your strategy! What do you do when you need to keep information secret? You could write it down using a secret code, or cipher. Here's one kind you can try.

**1.** Write your message in capital letters on two separate lines. Alternate each letter on different lines as shown:

SNEAK ALONG GARDEN FENCE = S E K L N G R E F N E
                                           N A A O G A D N E C

**2.** If needed, add an extra letter to the bottom line so each line has the same number of letters.

SNEAK ALONG GARDEN FENCE = S E K L N G R E F N E
                                           N A A O G A D N E C X

**3.** Next, write out the letters in line one and then line two in a single row. Break up the letters into groups to create nonsense words of different lengths.

SEK LNGR EF NENA A OGAD NECX

**4.** To solve the code, your friend will count the letters and divide them in half. Then he puts the first half on top and the second half underneath as you had them before.

SEK LNGR EF NE / NA A OGAD NECX    =    S E K L N G R E F N E
                                         N A A O G A D N E C X

**5.** Your friend can then rewrite the secret message by placing alternate letters together to form the words. He'll know to ignore any extra letters at the end.

S E K L N G R E F N E    =    SNEAK ALONG GARDEN FENCE
N A A O G A D N E C

# THE UNBREAKABLE CODE OF THE NAVAJO CODE TALKERS

Early in World War II (1939–1945), the Japanese were easily cracking codes used by the Allies. The United States recruited Navajo Indians to help create better codes. The Navajo language has no alphabet and is very hard to master. The Navajo "code talkers" used Navajo words to describe military terms. For example, the Navajo word *Jay-sho* means "buzzard." In the code, Jay-sho meant "bomber plane." The word for "turtle" meant "tank," and the word for "black sheep" meant "squad." Using this system, the Navajo could communicate complex messages in seconds—and enemies never cracked it.

# MAKE SOME MONEY

Want to earn some extra cash? Start your own business! Give your business a cool name and spread the word by making flyers and posters. You could even team up with a friend to make it more fun. Here are a few ideas to get you started.

## SELL VEGETABLES AND PLANTS

Order cheap seeds in the fall. Then plant them in pots and grow them indoors during the winter. In the spring you'll have plants to sell for a nice profit.

## CHORE SERVICE

Most everyone hates doing household chores. But chores aren't so bad when you're getting paid for them. Many people are willing to pay someone to do their housework for them.

## PET-SITTING OR DOG-WALKING

People love their furry friends. They'll often pay an honest and dependable person to take care of their pets when they're away from home.

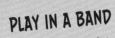

## PLAY IN A BAND

If you and your friends can play instruments, form a band. Learn some songs and put on some shows in the neighborhood. Rock on!

## LAWN AND SNOW SERVICE

You can make a lot of extra cash by mowing and raking people's lawns during the summer. During winter you can shovel snow off their driveways and sidewalks.

# BE A WRITER AND PUBLISHER

If you like to write stories, you can start a neighborhood magazine or newsletter to sell in your community. Is there an owl or woodpecker that lives in a nearby park? Take a picture and write a short piece for your magazine. Did someone on your block win a prize for the biggest pumpkin? Do an interview and write a story about it. You get the idea. People love to read about cool stuff going on in their area. If your newsletter becomes popular, you can make even more money by selling advertising space like big newspapers and magazines do.

# HOW ARE YOU SMART?

Being smart isn't just about doing well on tests and getting good grades. Some scientists believe people have at least eight different kinds of intelligence. Everyone has strengths and weaknesses in the various types of intelligence. Read about them below, and then see if you can recognize yourself in any of them.

## 1. VERBAL INTELLIGENCE

**SMART WITH WORDS.** People in this group might like to read, write, or do public speaking.

## 2. MUSICAL INTELLIGENCE

**SMART WITH MUSIC AND SOUNDS.** This group is talented at playing instruments and understanding music.

## 3. MATHEMATICAL INTELLIGENCE

**SMART WITH NUMBERS, PATTERNS, AND SCIENCE.** These people like mathematical puzzles, riddles, and doing science experiments.

## 4. VISUAL INTELLIGENCE

**SMART WITH IMAGES.** People who are visual often have artistic talents and skills such as drawing, painting, and designing things. They also often have a good sense of direction and are good at organizing things in small spaces.

## 5. BODY INTELLIGENCE

**PHYSICALLY SMART.** This group includes people who are good athletes and dancers. These people are also often good at fixing things and working with their hands.

## 6. INTERPERSONAL INTELLIGENCE

**SMART WITH PEOPLE AND SOCIAL SITUATIONS.**
People strong in this area often find it easy to relate to others. They are often seen as leaders and have lots of friends.

## 7. INTRAPERSONAL INTELLIGENCE

**SMART ABOUT YOURSELF.** These people know themselves well. They understand their own strengths and weaknesses. They're also good at thinking about the future and making goals for themselves.

## 8. NATURALIST INTELLIGENCE

**SMART ABOUT NATURE.** This group of people feels a strong connection to nature. They might be skilled at studying plants, animals, and the wilderness.

CREATIVITY

# EAT TO GET
# SMARTER

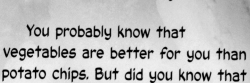

You probably know that vegetables are better for you than potato chips. But did you know that some foods are great for your brain as well as your body? These foods can help you focus on your work and manage your emotions. Look for foods that are filled with vitamins, protein, and healthy fats and oils.

Here are some great foods to help increase your energy and brainpower. Loading up on these superfoods instead of junk food can help you do better at school and in life.

- **OILY FISH:** Fish such as salmon and tuna are loaded with protein and healthy oils. They help keep your brain healthy so you can stay sharp and focused.

- **SEEDS AND NUTS:** Pistachios, walnuts, pumpkin seeds, sunflower seeds, and other seeds and nuts are loaded with protein and healthy fats. They make great snacks.

- **MILK:** Milk is full of calcium that helps strengthen your bones. It's also a terrific source of vitamins and protein.

- **EGGS:** Eggs are crammed full of vitamins, protein, iron, healthy fats, and more. They're good for your eyes and your brain, help prevent cancer and heart disease, and have several other health benefits.

- **COLORFUL VEGGIES:** Spinach, bell peppers, carrots, tomatoes, broccoli, and beets are all powerful vegetables. The more colorful they are, the more vitamins that are packed into them. Eat a variety of colorful veggies to get all the healthy vitamins your body needs.

Ever get hungry for an after-school snack? Want something to munch on during your next nature hike? Try out this healthy trail mix. It's loaded with good stuff to boost your energy and help you focus on your tasks instead of your stomach.

## HEALTHY TRAIL MIX

In a large bowl, mix together ½ cup (120-mL) of each of the following ingredients. After mixing, store in an airtight container for up to one month.

- raisins
- peanuts
- sunflower seeds
- dried fruit (cranberries, cherries, pineapple chunks, or banana chips)

- unsalted nuts (almonds, walnuts, pecans, or cashews)
- mini pretzels
- granola clusters
- chocolate chips, peanut butter chips, or candy-coated chocolates

# DO BETTER ON TESTS

Do you dread taking tests at school? Do you stay up late trying to cram every last fact into your brain? Stop worrying. Stressing out about tests won't help. Here are a few ways you can relax and have more confidence while taking tests.

## BEFORE THE TEST

Get a good night's sleep: Students need at least 10 hours of sleep a night. If you're sleepy, you won't be able to think clearly. Being tired can put you in a bad mood. This can lead to more stress and cause you to perform poorly on your test.

Study: That's a no-brainer, right? But don't wait until the last minute. Studying a little every day for several days is better than cramming everything in at the last minute.

Eat well: The day of the test, eat a healthy breakfast. Being hungry will keep you from thinking clearly and focusing on the test. Eggs are an excellent superfood loaded with brain-boosting protein.

Drink plenty of water: Keep your body and brain hydrated. If it's allowed, bring along a bottle of water to your test.

# DURING THE TEST

Chew gum: Studies show that chewing gum can help stimulate the part of your brain that remembers information.

Do belly breathing: Oxygen helps relieve stress and increases your ability to think clearly. Breathe in deeply and slowly through your nose as you expand your belly. Then breathe out slowly through your mouth.

Keep a positive attitude: Your attitude can affect how you feel about yourself. Stay positive and tell yourself things like, "I've studied, and I feel confident." Staying positive can help you stay calm and perform your best.

# Fact

Standardized testing became common in the United States by World War I (1914–1918). Automatic test scanning machines that read bubble sheets filled out by students were introduced in 1936.

# MAKE A
# STOP-MOTION
# MOVIE

Quiet on the set! Places, everyone! Lights ... Camera ... Action! Most guys love a fun movie. Whether you like adventure films, funny movies, or science fiction flicks, you can make your own using stop-motion animation. Follow the steps below to make your own blockbuster epic.

## STEP 1

### WRITE A STORY

Who is your story about? Invent a character and give him or her (or it) a problem to solve. Write it down so you can remember the details. For your first movie, keep it simple.

# STEP 2

## MAKE A SET AND CHARACTERS

It's time to choose what to use for your characters. You could use clay, paper cutouts, or action figures. Interlocking toys, such as LEGO® bricks, are popular for making stop-motion movies. The toy figures are simple to use, yet have enough detail to make realistic action.

Toy bricks are also handy for making cool sets. Everything stays nicely on the baseplates. You can also use clay, sticks, or rocks to make awesome sets for your story.

# STOP-MOTION MASTERS

Stop-motion was one of the first kinds of special effects used to make movies. Willis O'Brien used stop-motion to animate the giant gorilla in the 1933 film *King Kong*. From the 1950s to the 1990s, Ray Harryhausen became famous for his stop-motion work in films such as *Jason and the Argonauts* and *Clash of the Titans*. Harryhausen's work inspired many filmmakers of today. His influence is seen in many modern stop-motion movies such as the *Wallace and Gromit* films, *Paranorman*, and *The LEGO Movie*.

Wallace and Gromit

# STEP 3

## TAKE THE PHOTOS

You'll need a digital camera or a smartphone. If you have one, a tripod is useful for holding the camera steady. Set up your scene with your characters in it. Let's say you're animating a football game. Take a photo of the teams as they are lined up for a passing play. Then move the figures a little as if they are running on the field. Photograph the new positions. Then move the figures a tiny bit again and take another photo. Repeat this process several times until your scene is finished.

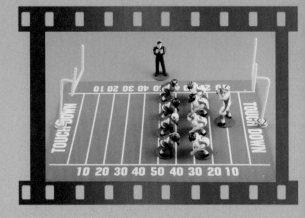

**TIP:** Experiment with a variety of angles, close-ups, and long-range shots. It can create different moods during the scene.

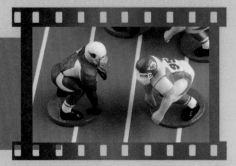

# STEP 4    ANIMATE

Load your photos onto a computer. Then use a movie-making program, such as iMovie, to put together your film. Load your photos into the computer program and tell it how many frames to use for each photo. A rate of three frames per photo is common.

# STEP 5

## ADD SOUND

If you want music, drag song files into the movie timeline. Or you can use a microphone to record speaking parts for your characters. You can also find free explosions and other sound effects to use in your film online. Once you're ready, click "play" and you'll be watching your very own stop-motion movie!

# STEP 6

## SHARE IT

You can share your movie with friends by posting it to a blog or on YouTube. As you get more practice, you can write more complicated stories and use different materials to make your movies.

# WHO'S MORE AWESOME?

## TONY HAWK

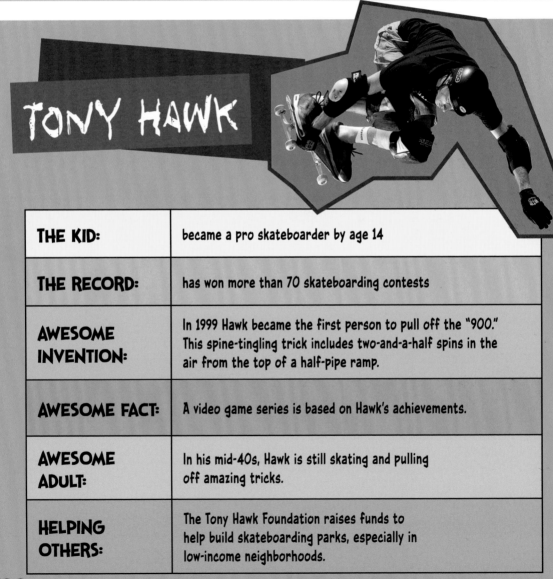

| THE KID: | became a pro skateboarder by age 14 |
|---|---|
| THE RECORD: | has won more than 70 skateboarding contests |
| AWESOME INVENTION: | In 1999 Hawk became the first person to pull off the "900." This spine-tingling trick includes two-and-a-half spins in the air from the top of a half-pipe ramp. |
| AWESOME FACT: | A video game series is based on Hawk's achievements. |
| AWESOME ADULT: | In his mid-40s, Hawk is still skating and pulling off amazing tricks. |
| HELPING OTHERS: | The Tony Hawk Foundation raises funds to help build skateboarding parks, especially in low-income neighborhoods. |

A lot of guys have achieved amazing things during their lives. However, the guys listed here accomplished more things as young men than many people do in their entire lives. And even as adults, their adventures show that growing up doesn't mean you have to stop being awesome!

# RICHARD BRANSON

| THE KID: | Branson began a magazine called *Student* at age 16. When he was 22, he founded Virgin Records, one of the most successful record companies of all time. |
|---|---|
| THE RECORD: | at age 60, became the oldest person to kitesurf across the English Channel |
| AWESOME INVENTION: | founded the company Virgin Galactic to build spaceships for carrying tourists into space |
| AWESOME FACT: | crossed both the Atlantic Ocean and Pacific Ocean in a hot air balloon |
| AWESOME ADULT: | planning to do the first manned dive to the Puerto Rico Trench, the deepest spot in the Atlantic Ocean |
| HELPING OTHERS: | has given millions of dollars to charities to fight disease and global warming |

# DEAL WITH
## STICKY SITUATIONS

### How to Handle Bullying

If someone is bullying you on the bus, at school, at the local park, or on the Internet, you need to deal with it. It's never OK for someone to make you feel scared or unsafe. Try these ideas to deal with someone who likes to pick on you or others.

**IGNORE HIM.** Most people bully because they want others to cry, act scared, or get upset. But if you play it cool, many times the bullying will stop.

**STAND UP TO HIM.** If someone is bullying you, he usually won't expect you to stand up to him. Sometimes just telling him, loud and clear, to knock it off will do the trick. Act brave and strong, even if you don't feel that way.

**ESCAPE.** If you feel you are in danger, run away as quickly as you can and find an adult.

**GET AN ADULT TO HELP.** If you tried to stop the bullying, but it didn't work, you need to get help from someone in charge. If you're at school, talk to a teacher, principal, or counselor. Outside of school you can share the problem with a parent or another adult you trust.

# How to Resolve a Conflict

IF A COUPLE OF YOUR FRIENDS ARE ARGUING, YOU CAN HELP THEM TO TALK IT OUT. OFFER TO MEDIATE THE CONFLICT. THAT MEANS YOU'LL WORK WITH THEM TO SOLVE THE PROBLEM IN A WAY THAT WORKS FOR EVERYONE. HERE ARE SOME TIPS ON HOW TO HELP RESOLVE AN ARGUMENT.

**Let each person talk:** Ask the guys to take turns talking about how they feel and what they want. Don't let them interrupt, attack, or accuse each other. This is a time for each person to show respect for the other's feelings.

**Summarize the situation:** Repeat the problem back to them as you see it. Describe the solutions that each person would like to see.

**Brainstorm solutions:** Each person should take some time to think about different ways to solve the problem. The solutions need to address what each person wants. Remind your friends that they will probably need to make a compromise.

**Agree on a solution:** Choose a solution that works best for everyone. It should be something your friends will each mostly like, but will not make them 100 percent happy. That's how compromise works.

**Help put the solution into action:** Actions speak louder than words. Make an effort to make sure the compromise works. For example, if your friends' argument is about sharing video game time, offer to track the time of each player's turn.

# MAKE YOUR ROOM AWESOME

You spend a lot of time in your room. You sleep there. You spend time with friends there. And you probably do your homework there. You may as well make it a cool place to hang out that also reflects your personality. Here are some ideas to help make your room an awesome space. To be safe, get an adult to help you with some of the building projects.

## USE VERTICAL SPACE
Give yourself more room by putting up high shelves, hooks, or stacked cubbies where you can store your stuff.

## PAINT
Ask a parent if you can paint one or more of your walls a fun color. You could even paint a picture on a wall or get some cool wall stickers.

## PUT UP ART
Designate a wall for your awesome photos or posters. Original artwork by you or your friends is unique and totally personal.

## USE MOOD LIGHTING
Table lamps create more comfortable lighting than overhead lights. Try using orange or red lightbulbs, or get a lava lamp to give your room a funky look.

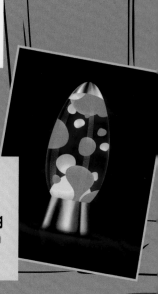

**SET UP A SPECIAL AREA** If you have enough space, set aside part of the room as a workspace. You can use it for doing homework or a hobby such as building models or creating your stop-motion movie.

**DECORATE**
There are tons of different items you can use to decorate your room. Consider adding a unique wall clock, cool sculptures, or weird plants.

**CHANGE THE SURFACE**
Try to find a cool rug for the floor or a fun bedspread for your bed.

**TURN UP THE TUNES**
No room is complete without a few tunes to liven things up. Set up an MP3 player or radio to listen to your favorite music.

# KEEP YOUR STUFF PRIVATE

Does your little brother or sister snoop around in your room when you're not there? Your siblings will respect your space if you talk to them maturely. Be clear that you want them to stay out of your stuff. And let them know that you'll respect their space too. Be respectful and you'll earn respect in return. Of course, if necessary, you may need to find a way to keep your things private. Get a file box or a desk that you can keep locked to keep prying eyes away from your stuff.

# SPOOK YOUR SIBLING

Is Halloween your favorite holiday? Or maybe you like April Fools' Day. Either way, this harmless trick is a great way to scare the wits out of your kid brother or sister. You can use this sneaky science trick to spook your parents too!

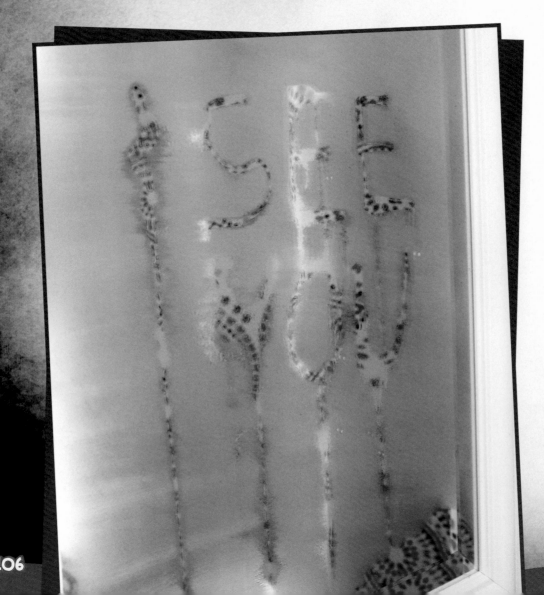

## HERE'S WHAT YOU NEED:

- a cotton swab
- a glass of water
- liquid dish soap

**Step 1:** Mix a few drops of liquid soap into the water so it dissolves.

**Step 2:** Just before your brother or sister goes to take a hot shower, take the soap solution and cotton swab to the bathroom.

**Step 3:** Using the cotton swab like a pen, write a haunting or funny message on the bathroom mirror. The words will be invisible on the mirror. Keep dipping your swab in the soap solution to keep it wet.

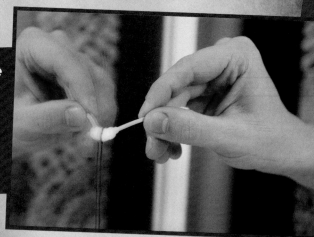

**Step 4:** Quickly sneak out and get rid of the evidence. Dump out the soap solution and throw away the cotton swabs. Then wait for the fun to start.

**Step 5:** When your brother or sister gets into the shower, be sure the bathroom door is closed so the steam stays inside. As the mirror fogs up, your secret message will appear on it. When your victim gets out of the shower, he or she will see your spooky message!

# KEEP YOUR BIKE IN TIP-TOP SHAPE

Your bike is important! It's probably one of the most expensive things you own. It may also be the only transportation you can use without an adult. You need to take good care of it. Follow these tips to help keep your bike in great shape.

**KEEP IT DRY** Store your bike indoors so it's not exposed to the weather. Moisture can cause rust and ruin any moving parts. If you can't store it inside, get a tarp to cover it. After riding in the rain, be sure to wipe down your bike to dry it.

**KEEP IT CLEAN** You don't need to use soap, which can cause rust. But wipe down your bike with a damp cloth when it's dirty. If it's covered in mud, spray it down with a hose first. Pay special attention to moving parts, especially the chain. Sand and dirt can ruin it. Use a *stiff* brush to clean the grime off of the chain. Don't forget to dry off your bike after cleaning it.

### LUBRICATE THE CHAIN

Use a special bicycle lubricant, being careful to cover every inch of the chain. Hold a cloth under the chain as you apply the lubricant. This will keep the slick stuff off the ground and your brakes, which could prevent them from working well. Do this about once a week if you're a regular rider.

### KEEP THE TIRES FIRM

Check your tire pressure before every ride. The proper pressure is often found on the sidewall of the tires. But most tires need pressure of about 75 pounds per square inch. Use a pressure gauge if you have one. Otherwise, you can pump up the tires until they feel nice and hard.

### WATCH THE BRAKES

Check your brake pads every month or so to be sure they're not too worn down. If they're getting thin, it's time to replace them. Also be sure they contact the rim of the wheels and not the tires.

If you can squeeze the brake lever all the way down, you need to tighten the cable. Squeeze the brake calipers together to release the cable. Then use an Allen wrench or bike tool to loosen the nut on the brake caliper. Pull about 1/8 inch (0.32 centimeter) of cable through. Then tighten the nut and reattach the cable. Test the brake lever to see how the brakes respond. If they still feel loose, repeat the process as needed until they work correctly.

# INDEX

Published by Capstone Press,
1710 Roe Crest Drive, North Mankato, Minnesota 56003
www.capstoneyoungreaders.com

**Library of Congress Cataloging-in-Publication Data**
Braun, Eric, 1971–
The guys' guide to making life more awesome / by Eric Braun.
pages cm—(Capstone young readers)
Includes index.
Summary: "Describes various trivia, tips, activities, and other useful information for making sports, the outdoors, cities, and daily life more fun and interesting"—Provided by publisher.
ISBN 978-1-62370-060-7 (paperback)
1. Boys—Life skills guides—Juvenile literature. I. Title.
HQ775.B665 2014
305.230811—dc23                                                          2013045997

**Editorial Credits**
Aaron Sautter, editor; Veronica Scott, designer; Eric Gohl, media researcher;
Jennifer Walker, production specialist

**Photo Credits**
**Alamy:** FLPA, 70 (lynx scat), Gary Cook, 70 (wolf scat), Joe Blossom, 70 (beaver scat), North Wind Picture Archives, 30b, Rafael Ben-Ari, 74, Simon Colmer, 70 (fox scat), tbkmedia.de, 44b; **AP Photo:** 20r, Gene Puskar, 22b; **BigStockPhoto.com:** SURZ, 68; **Capstone:** 11b, 16b, 18l, 19 (all), 29b, 34, 62, 63b, 64, 75, Fernando Cano, 17 (all); **Capstone Studio:** Karon Dubke, 35, 65, 77 (fishing rod), 92–93bgd, 93b, 96 (football toy), 97t, 98–99 (all), 106, 107; **Corbis:** Reuters/Luke MacGregor, 101; **Courtesy of artofmanliness.com:** 9 (illustrations); **Dreamstime:** Linda Morland, 45b, Martin Ellis, 26r, Naci Yavuz, 27l, Rolf52, 56bl, Scott Anderson, 21b, Sean Pavone, 39t, Thomas Vieth, 48, Valentin Armianu, 57t; **Getty Images:** AFP/Denis Charlet, 39m, Allsport/Robert Cianflone, 69, Elsa, 23t, European School, 54m, Flickr Vision/John Dillon, 47t, PhotoQuest, 87, SSPL, 39b; **iStockphotos:** Mike Rodriguez, 8t, Sieto, 70 (bear scat), Whiteway, 70 (hare scat); **Library of Congress:** 81b; **Newscom:** Album/Dreamworks, 97b, EPA/John G. Mabanglo, 25bl/br, Everett Collection, 54b, Mirrorpix/Daily Mirror, 56br, Reuters/Darren Staples, 9tr, Reuters/Doug Kapustin, 8b, Splash News, 78, ZUMA Press/Vaughn Youtz, 100; **Shutterstock:** 1973kla, 2m/b, Aigars Reinholds, 89b, Aleks Melnik, 14l, 15, 20l, 91 (ball & microphone), Alena Hovorkova, 90 (doodles), Anastasiia Kucherenko, 102 (all), Anatolich, 67 (cricket), Anikakodydkova, 52m, Anthony Correia, 26l, Artex67, 86, attaphong, 63t, Attitude, 3 (bear), Audrey Snider-Bell, 82b, 83b, AVA Bitter, 80t, Barnaby Chambers, 109tl, 109b, Big Pants Production, 83t, Bikeworldtravel, 38t, bioraven, 6, BONNINSTUDIO, 105t, Brandon Alms, 67 (firefly), Brian Lasenby, 66 (prickly pear), buttet, 85t, Catalin Petolea, 60f, CoolR, 30t, cristapper, 37tr, Danielbotha, 108l, Danussa, 3bgd, 38–39bgd, 46–47bgd, 50–51bgd, 52–53bgd, Dariush M, 88bl, Dariusz Majgier, 67 (tick), Decha Thapanya, 67 (blister beetle), Denis Semenchenko, 105b, digidreamgrafix, 51m, Dmitry Naumov, 51b, dotshock, 89t, Dr. Morley Read, 73bl, Elinalee, 94–95bgd, Eric Broder Van Dyke, 37tl, Eric Isselee, 54t, Fernando Cortes, 37br, fotosub, 66 (acorn), Galyna Andrushko, 58–59, George Muresan, 85b, geraria, 70 (illustrated fox), hin255, 42t, hjakkal, 25 (basketball hoop), hxdyl, 56m, Hyde Peranitti, 67 (caterpillar), Igor Yanovskiy, cover, iko, 66 (mushroom), Jacek Chabraszewski, 52b, Jan Mika, 109tr, JENG_NIAMWHAN, 66 (wild rice), jennyt, 43t, Jun Mu, 41b, JSlavy, 16t, Kaliva, 24, Kathy Gold, 31br, Kenneth Keifer, 66 (hemlock), khandisha, 10 (bicycling gear), 11tl, 12 (bicycling gear), 13t, kstudija, 10 (silhouettes), KUCO, 90 (cello player), Kudryashka, 92–93bgd (food doodles), Leonard Zhukovsky, 38b, LHF Graphics, 27r, littleny, 49b, locote, 7, 12 (bicyclist), makar, 91 (tree), MaKars, 41t, Marie C Fields, 56t, MARKABOND, 51t, Matt Knoth, 40, Mayovskyy Andrew, 45tr, Merggy, 95, mhatzapa, 22t, 28t, Microstock Man, 60–61, Migel, 53, Mihai-Bogdan Lazar, 45tl, mir_vam, 11tr, mironov, 76–77bgd, Mitch Gunn, 21t, Monkey Business Images, 52t, 88t, Mur34, 23b, Nagy-Bagoly Arpad, 66 (blackberries), Naira Kalantaryan, 44t, Neyro, 25 (basketball), Ortodox, 67 (maggot), Oxygen64, 96–97 (film reel), Petr Jilek, 43b, Photo House, 71, Pinkyone, 4, Pirha, 91 (drawing hand), plasid, 66 (rosary peas), plastique, 88br, Potapov Alexander, 71, PRILL, 49t, prizzz, 66 (baneberries), Radu Bercan, 37bl, Rahhal, 57m, Rudy Umans, 108r, ranker, 28b, 29t, Rednaxel, 18r, Sandy Stupart, 36l, Scotshot, 46, Scott E Read, 72, Seamartini Graphics, 77 (fish), Serg64, 67 (fly), Sergey Nivens, 84b, Sergeypykhonin, 14r, Sign N Symbol Production, 82t, Smileus, 66 (poisonous nuts), smuay, 67 (termite), Spirit of America, 47m, Stealh, 67 (grasshopper), Steshkin Yevgeniy, 67 (earthworms), Stuart Monk, 57b, Suzanne Tucker, 84t, Tatiana Volgutova, 66 (cattails), Tony Campbell, 42b, Tribalium, 66 (illustrated reeds), TTphoto, 70 (moose scat), Tupungato, 32–33, Tyler Olson, 70 (deer scat), Vinata, 104–105bgd, Visun Khankasem, 47b, Volodymyr Burdiak, 73t, Voropaev Vasiliy, 31bl, WDG Photo, 36r, yienkeat, 67 (illustrated trees), Yourthstock, 73br, Yu Lan, 2t, zayats-and-zayats, 104, zeber, 13b, 108–109bgd, Zlatko Guzmic, 35bgd, 49bgd; **SuperStock:** Animals Animals, 70 (raccoon scat); **Wikipedia:** Jami Dwyer, 79, Mahanga, 31t, Public Domain, 80b, 81t

**Design Elements:** Shutterstock

Printed in the United States of America in Brainerd, Minnesota
092013     007776BANGS14